GENDER AS CALLING

The
Gospel
&
Gender
Identity

A Testimony of the
Reformed Presbyterian Church of North America

Crown & Covenant
PUBLICATIONS

7408 Penn Avenue
Pittsburgh, Pa., 15208

©2017
Crown & Covenant Publications and
The Synod of the Reformed Presbyterian Church of North America

Second Printing, 2019

This report, which was originally published in the *2017 Minutes of the Synod of the Reformed Presbyterian Church of North America*, has been copyedited for book publishing and may differ in minor aspects from the original. Every effort by the publisher has been made to reproduce the original report with accuracy.

Printed in the United States of America

ISBN: 978-1-943017-12-6 (paperback)
ISBN: 978-1-943017-13-3 (ebook)

Library of Congress Control Number: 2017953267

Arno Pro was used for the body text and headers.

Contents

Preface

It is stunning how rapidly the transgender movement has gained mainstream acceptance in Western society. It took more than a century for the homosexual movement to win cultural affirmation.[1] Transgenderism's acceptance happened much more speedily, partly due to the path carved out by the homosexuality movement.

National Review correspondent Kevin D. Williamson compares the two movements: "Thirty years passed between the American Psychiatric Association's 1973 decision to remove homosexuality as a mental disorder from its *Diagnostic and Statistical Manual* and homosexuals' arrival as a protected 14th Amendment class in *Lawrence* [*v. Texas*, in 2003]. The time lapse between the APA's removal of 'gender-identity disorder'...and the emergence of transgender people as a protected class under civil-rights law as interpreted by the Obama administration: three years."[2] The speed of transgenderism's emergence into the mainstream has left many Christians scrambling to make sense of the movement. In this booklet, it is our desire to contribute toward a careful engagement with the transgender movement's claims, drawing upon thinking that is rooted in biblical teaching and biblical compassion (Prov. 12:17–18; Eph. 4:15).

This booklet begins with an introduction to the development of the transgender movement and its terminology (chapter I). In chapter II, we will critique two philosophies that have been widely embraced in western thought and which undergird the transgender movement, but which, we will argue, are unbiblical. The rest of the booklet will offer what we believe to be a biblical response to transgenderism. This part of the argument begins with a biblically grounded vision for gender (chapter III). We will argue that gender is a *calling* the individual receives in his or her anatomical constitution; gender should not be viewed as an identity rooted in one's psyche (or brain). This argument leaves open the question of gender for those born with anatomical gender ambiguity. Therefore, a further chapter of this booklet will address the special questions associated with such cases of anatomical ambiguity (chapter IV). The booklet will close with a chapter offering advice for faithful, pastoral ministry in the face of transgenderism and for those dealing with transgender self-perceptions (chapter V).

—*The Synod of the Reformed Presbyterian Church of North America*

I

Key Concepts and Terminology

A person's sex/gender has both a physical dimension and a social dimension. The physical identity "male" or "female" refers to an individual's sexual, medical, and reproductive traits. The social identity "male" or "female" refers to the individual's fitness for certain roles in society, especially those of husband/wife and father/mother. Traditionally, a person's physical sex and social gender were regarded as unified. To be physically male was, of necessity, to be socially male also. But today, this traditional perspective has been challenged. It is now common to distinguish physical maleness/femaleness as a person's *sex*, while the term *gender* refers to the individual's social (and psychological) identity. Furthermore, an individual's sex and gender are no longer regarded as necessarily matching. A person might be sexed as a male and gendered as a female, or vice versa. It is evident that a person's sex and gender match in most instances, but this tendency is now regarded as a statistical norm rather than a definitive norm. The terms *sex* and *gender* have therefore taken on distinct nuance in modern discourse:[3]

> Sex—refers to the *biological* classification of a person as boy/man or girl/woman (or in some cases as hermaphrodite/intersex) based on physiological features. Some physiological markers are considered *primary sex characteristics* (i.e., anatomical features identified with reproduction, such as genitalia, gonads, and reproductive organs). Other physiological features are considered *secondary sex characteristics*

(e.g., enlarged breasts and wider hips in women; facial hair, deeper voice, and greater muscle mass in men). At a deeper, less visible level biological factors are sometimes identified as markers of a person's sex, such as certain hormones (androgens are typically regarded as "male sex hormones" while estrogen and progesterone are generally viewed as "female sex hormones")[4] and the presence of certain chromosome pairings (XY for men and XX for women).

Gender—refers to the *psychological* and *social* classification of a person as male or female (or in some cases as androgynous/"genderqueer"). This identification is now said to be determined from one's self-perception with respect to socially recognized traits and roles of males and females. Sometimes a further distinction is drawn between an individual's *gender identity* (his or her self-perception as being gendered male or female) and that same individual's *gender role* (whether the person actually adopts a male or female role in the community).

Now that sex and gender are no longer regarded as necessarily matched, terms have been coined to mark those whose sex and gender do or do not match. The term *cisgender* [SIS-jen-dər] refers to those whose gender and sex do match. The term *transgender* refers to those whose sex and gender do not match. Thus, a person born with the physical traits of a male, and who also identifies psychologically and socially as a male, is *cisgender*; but a person born with the physical features of a male who identifies socially as female, is considered *transgender*.

Some studies indicate that transgenderism is experienced by between 1 in 10,000 to 13,000 adult males and between 1 in 20,000 to 34,000 adult females.[5] Until recently, the American Psychiatric Association (APA) instructed medical health professionals to diagnose this experience as "Gender Identity Disorder."[6] However, the latest update to the *Diagnostic and Statistical Manual of Mental Disorders* (DSM-5) has removed this diagnosis as a disorder. Instead, the new DSM provides the more narrowly targeted designation, "Gender Dysphoria." Under this new designation, transgender identity is itself affirmed as a healthy condition (it is not a "disorder"); it is only the distress that one sometimes experiences from being transgender that is unhealthy ("gender dysphoria"). *Gender dysphoria* is defined as an experience of clinically significant distress due to a "marked incongruence between one's experienced/expressed gender and assigned gender, of at least 6 months' duration."[7]

Now that gender nonconformity is regarded as normal (if statistically rare): the goal of treatment is no longer to resolve the sense of being transgender, but to resolve psychological discomfort with one's transgender identity. "Gender nonconformity is not in itself a mental disorder," the APA now states, "The critical element of gender dysphoria is the presence of clinically significant distress associated with the condition."[8]

The APA considered removing reference to gender nonconformity altogether, just as homosexuality was depathologized by its removal from the 1973 edition of the DSM (there is no "gay dysphoria" entry in the DSM). However, the diagnosis "gender dysphoria" was provided to ensure that insurance companies would cover treatment from distress related to transgenderism, which treatment can be quite costly particularly if it involves surgery. According to the APA, "Persons experiencing gender dysphoria need a diagnostic term that protects their access to care and won't be used against them in social, occupational, or legal areas. When it comes to access to care, many of the treatment options for this condition include counseling, cross-sex hormones, gender reassignment surgery, and social and legal transition to the desired gender. To get insurance coverage for the medical treatments, individuals need a diagnosis."[9] There are efforts, nonetheless, pressing the APA to depathologize gender nonconformity altogether, allowing for clinical levels of distress arising from gender issues to be diagnosed and treated under other psychological categories (such as depression).[10]

On the other hand, there are those who question the condition's hasty removal from classification as a psychological "disorder." Both the etiology and effective treatment for this condition remain elusive, justifying concern whether depathologizing the condition is actually medically warranted or if this move was a response to cultural pressures. Oliver O'Donovan represents these concerns with two points of criticism:

> First, the questionable appropriateness of surgery to bring a healthy body into conformity with the demands of a psychological disorder, [which is] a paradoxical use of the healing art; secondly, the questionable long-term benefit to the patients. There are conflicting claims as to the measure of improvement in psychological and social welfare that can be expected from the change of gender role. Studies indicate a

high vulnerability to depression in postoperative transsexuals; [and] a disturbing minority of patients desire to return to their original sex-role.[11]

Another important voice of concern is that of Paul McHugh, psychiatrist-in-chief at Johns Hopkins University when he helped lead and then eventually shut down the gender identity clinic at that institution. Paul McHugh appointed a colleague (Jon Meyer) to conduct follow-up research on gender reassignment surgeries conducted at Johns Hopkins, and explains the results: "He found that most of the patients he tracked down some years after their surgery were contented with what they had done and that only a few regretted it. But in every other respect, they were little changed in their psychological condition. They had much the same problems with relationships, work, and emotions as before. The hope that they would emerge now from their emotional difficulties to flourish psychologically had not been fulfilled. We saw the results as demonstrating that just as these men enjoyed cross-dressing as women before the operation so they enjoyed cross-living after it. But they were no better in their psychological integration or any easier to live with. With these facts in hand I concluded that Hopkins was fundamentally cooperating with a mental illness. We psychiatrists, I thought, would do better to concentrate on trying to fix their minds and not their genitalia."[12] Elsewhere, McHugh has compared the surgical treatment of otherwise healthy bodies based on confused gender perception as analogous to providing liposuction to individuals who are persuaded they are overweight when, in fact, suffering from anorexia or other psychological imbalances that distort their accurate perception of themselves.[13] Not all researchers in the field share McHugh's conclusions about post-operative problems. A number of recent studies suggest that sex reassignment surgeries and hormonal therapies may lead to positive outcomes more often than represented by O'Donovan and McHugh and the studies they cite.[14] Some recent studies indicate mixed results.[15] From a strictly medical perspective, advances in technique may improve post-operative satisfaction levels, but the effectiveness—and the morality—of sex reassignment surgery remains controversial.

While *sex* is now regarded as a physical identity and *gender* as a social construct, the distinction is not always cut-and-dry. First of all, there are instances where anatomical features are sexually ambiguous, as when a child is born with mixed or indeterminate genitalia. These conditions are unusual, but less rare than many realize. Such persons were historically identified as *hermaphrodites* and more recently as *intersex* or as persons with *Disorders of Sex Development* (DSD).[16] This terminology is presently in flux, as experts seek to determine the labels that offer the greatest help and least stigma for these conditions.[17] (This booklet will use the term *intersex* as one of the least stigmatizing among presently available options.) Thus, the identification of physical sex is not always straightforward.

Additionally, modern neuroscience is typically materialist, and therefore even a psychological perception of gender is ultimately regarded as the product of biology. From this perspective, gender is fundamentally physiological as well. Many researchers suspect that gender perception may arise from the biology of the brain, holding to what is commonly called the Brain-Sex Theory. Dick Swaab and Alicia Garcia-Falgueras of the Netherlands Institute for Neuroscience explain the basic theory, thus: "During the intrauterine period the fetal brain develops in the male direction through a direct action of testosterone on the developing nerve cells, or in the female direction through the absence of this hormone surge. In this way, our gender identity (the conviction of belonging to the male or female gender) and sexual orientation are programmed into our brain structures when we are still in the womb. However, since sexual differentiation of the genitals [which is also determined by testosterone levels] takes place in the first two months of pregnancy and sexual differentiation of the brain starts in the second half of pregnancy, these two processes can be influenced independently, which may result in transsexuality."[18] In other words, if there is a high level of testosterone present during the early stages of fetal development but for some reason a sharp decline in testosterone levels later in development, a child might form with male genitalia but a brain possessing neural characteristics more typical of a female. Evidence supporting this thesis is still limited,[19] but the supposition ought not be dismissed out of hand.

One of the most notable studies into Brain-Sex Theory was published in 1995 by a team of researchers led by Jiang-Ning Zhou at the Netherlands Institute for Brain Research. Zhou and his team examined the hypothalami of six male-to-female transsexuals. The researchers focused particularly on an area of the brain known as BSTc (i.e., "the central subdivision of the bed nucleus of the stria terminalis"). BSTc is "a brain area that is essential for sexual behaviour, [and] is larger in men than in women." But in this study, "a female-sized BSTc was found in male-to-female transsexuals."[20] Could this indicate the possession of an anatomically "female" brain by certain persons with a male body, and vice versa? Critics have suggested that these findings might result from hormone therapy utilized by the six individuals included in that study, rather than indicating a causal brain feature.[21] Nevertheless, additional studies seem to strengthen the hypothesis that biological features of the brain may correlate with an individual's perception of gender.[22] This line of research further indicates that the modern distinction, "sex is physical/ gender is social," may not be so cut-and-dry.

The terms and concepts discussed so far indicate the decoupling of anatomical sex from social/psychological gender. Nevertheless, many of these trends continue to operate within a basic understanding of sex/gender as binary. A person is anatomically male or female, and gendered as male or female. However, another complexity in the discussion is captured by the terms *genderqueer* and *genderfluid*.

"Most of us are used to the idea of two sexes," writes Michigan State University scholar Alice Domurat Dreger, "and most of us are used to being only one....But the fact is that not everybody arrives in this world ready to be squeezed into one or the other generally accepted *anatomic* patterns of what we usually think of as male and female...."[23] In other words, the binary categories of *male* and *female* may be derived from the most common configurations of human sexuality, but they do not adequately account for all of the configurations of human anatomy. Therefore, it is sometimes said that the binary model of gender ought to be blurred into a continuum or abandoned altogether. Some individuals prefer to identify as *genderqueer* or *genderfluid*.

The term *genderqueer* conveys the idea that one does not identify as either male or female. Within a *genderqueer* conception, gender is viewed as a continuum with "maleness" and "femaleness" on the two poles of that continuum. Individuals adopting a *genderqueer* identity regard themselves as located at various points along that continuum, with some more male traits and some more female traits. A person who identifies as *genderqueer* sometimes prefers to use gender neutral pronouns. Traditional, non-gendered pronouns like "one" or "they" may be used, or newly coined gender-neutral pronouns such as "ze" and "hir." (*Ze* is a gender-neutral equivalent of he/she, [pronounced *zē*]; *hir* is a gender-neutral equivalent of him/her, [pronounced *hēr*].)[24] The term *genderfluid* is sometimes used synonymously with *genderqueer*, although *genderfluid* can refer more precisely to a person who regards gender as adaptable throughout life. A genderfluid individual may fluctuate between the male and female poles on the gender continuum, without being fixed to any particular category at any given time. These latter terms reveal some of the inconsistencies regarding the validity or invalidity of binary sex/gender categories still being fleshed out within the transgender movement.

It is typically transgender activists who uphold the binary, male/female categories who also promote sex-change surgery to bring the anatomical sex of a transgender individual into greater alignment with his or her perceived gender. Not all would regard the alignment of sex and gender as important; but it is among transgender activists who uphold the binary construct of sex and gender that corrective treatments like surgery are most likely to be promoted. Thus, for example, Chaz Bono has said, "There's a gender in your brain and a gender in your body. For 99 percent of people, those things are in alignment. For transgender people, they're mismatched. That's all it is. It's not complicated, it's not a neurosis. It's a mix-up. It's a birth defect, like a cleft palate."[25] However, there are those who insist Chaz Bono's way of thinking is misguided and that the binary framework ought to be rejected, altogether. These would balk at Bono's characterization of female feelings inside a male body as "a birth defect." The *genderqueer* perspective argues that such stereotypes about "right" and "wrong" alignments between psychological and physical traits should be abandoned, altogether. Within this latter perspective: sex-reassignment surgery is a matter of personal freedom, but not the correction of a defect.

Clearly, the transgender movement is as complicated as the varied experiences of those who are part of it. We must be careful not to presume that there is a stereotypical transgender-identified individual, or that the frustrations and excitements which this movement represents are monolithic. The varied vocabulary of the movement captures its complexity.[26]

II

Philosophical Presuppositions

Even though the mainstream acceptance of transgenderism is quite recent, there are longstanding philosophical influences in western society that undergird this acceptance. Two of these philosophies are *existentialism* and *Cartesian mind-body dualism* (cf., gnosticism). Those are not terms that roll easily off the tongue. These are not philosophical ideas people commonly talk about. Nevertheless, they are philosophies which have profoundly influenced western thought, and upon which transgenderism's cultural acceptability depends. In other words, our response to the transgender movement will follow on two levels. In this chapter, we want to address the philosophical underpinnings that lead to a social acceptance of transgenderism. Then, in the following chapter, we will offer a biblical doctrine of gender and its implications for transgenderism.

The first of these philosophical influences we will critique is *existentialism*. The foundational doctrine of existentialism is that "existence precedes essence."[27] Existentialism posits that a person's identity (or, essence) is rooted in his or her existence as experienced. Jean-Paul Sartre (one of the founding fathers of existentialism) explained the meaning of this doctrine with the following illustration: "If we consider a manufactured object, such as...a paper knife [i.e., a letter opener], we note that this object was produced by a craftsman who drew his inspiration from a concept....The essence of the paper knife—that is, the sum formulae and properties that enable it to be produced and defined—precedes its existence."[28] In cases of manufacture, essence (i.e., the nature of a thing) precedes existence (i.e., particular things). Sartre's illustration captures the basis for a Christian view of humankind as beings created according to a divine pattern, the features of which (including human gender categories) are revealed in God's Word. Sartre rightly notes that, in a Christian worldview, "Man possesses a human nature; this 'human nature,' which is the concept of that which is human, is found in all men.... [But] atheistic existentialism ... states that if God does not exist ... there is no human nature since there is no God to conceive of it.... Man is nothing other than what he makes of himself."[29] Existentialism has thus loosed personal meaning from God's design;[30] it has relocated personal meaning within the *anxiety* of radical self-determination ("anxiety" being the term invoked by the founders of the movement).[31]

Early existentialists focused on the rejection of divinely imposed *moral* categories, promoting self-determination free from religiously imposed definitions of morality. However, existentialism also renounces the absolute value of *social* categories. One recent consequence has been the rejection of sex and gender as being divinely authoritative categories. Al Mohler notes, "One of the central tenets of [existentialist] postmodernism is that 'reality' itself is socially constructed....The transgender revolution would have been impossible without this postmodern development, for the idea of gender as a socially constructed reality is indispensable to the transgender worldview."[32] A person's gender is now said to be existentially identified, rather than (as we will argue) being "read" in the body and responded to as a divine calling.

Within the existentialist worldview, social categories like gender are not necessarily ignored, but they are regarded as humanly constructed conventions which may be more or less useful. For example, Alice Domurat Dreger writes, "Come to think of it, why bother labeling males, females, and hermaphrodites? Part of the reason is that it is important to know about one's own body [esp. the kinds of processes and illnesses to which one is prone based on given anatomical features]....But a large part of the reason for sex-sorting is that we make very important social distinctions based on malehood and femalehood [such as the roles of 'mother' and 'father']."[33] In other words, the categories *male* and *female* can have medical and social usefulness; but they are merely descriptive tools invented by society.

This demotion of gender categories from prescriptive norms to descriptive tools would make sense if the basis for defining those categories is the observation of actual persons (i.e., if "existence precedes essence"). Indeed, if gender categories ("essence") are just an attempt to make sense of humans as they exist in the world ("existence"), then the binary system of male and female actually ignores a significant number of persons whose physiological gender traits are ambiguous or complicated. If existentialism were correct and "existence precedes essence," then the church would need to take her place at the forefront of the transgender movement pursuing the affirmation of categories outside of the traditional binary. But we are compelled by Scripture to reject the existentialist premise, and to maintain instead that unified sex-gender categories are divinely appointed vocations to which individuals are called (see chapter III).

Biblical Christianity encourages persons to explore their unique gifts and personality traits, with great freedom in doing so. But, we are to nurture our unique interests and inclinations within the authoritative categories appointed for us by our Maker, including the call to serve God and others as "cisgender" men or women. This commitment does not deny the real experience of many whose anatomy is ambiguous or whose personality (and even brain biology) may seem to fit the typical experiences of the opposite sex. A Christian worldview must find ways to address the real men and women and boys and girls whose experiences do not fit obviously or neatly into typical gender experiences. Nevertheless, if the Bible is truly a divinely inspired record of the Creator's purposes for humankind, then we must insist that "essence precedes existence" and individual meaning ought to be nurtured—and enabled to flourish—within the binary and unified sex/gender categories appointed by our Maker. This biblical view of human nature (that essence precedes existence) provides different guidance for responding to a perceived sex/gender "mismatch" than that offered by a culture steeped in existentialist ideals (that existence precedes essence). We will further explore this alternative, biblical response in the next chapter of this booklet.

A second unbiblical notion which pervades western culture, and which has become an important basis for the popular embrace of transgenderism, is *Cartesian mind-body dualism*. According the French philosopher René Descartes (1596–1650), the human being is constituted by two *distinct* substances: the mind or soul and the body. For Descartes, "the soul [is] the true substantial form of man" which inhabits the body.[34] Thus, a person's identity is defined by his or her soul; the body is of secondary relevance to the person's identity. Traditional Christian orthodoxy agrees with the identification of human nature as comprised of both body and soul;[35] however, there are seeds of serious error within the Cartesian preeminence of the soul to the neglect of regard for the body as a real part of the person's "true substantial form." Christopher West counters this tendency, explaining, "In the biblical understanding, there exists a profound unity between that which is physical and that which is spiritual. This means that our bodies are not mere shells in which our true 'spiritual selves' live. We are a profound unity of body and soul, matter and spirit. In a very real way, we *are* our bodies."[36] In fact, when it comes to the question of gender, we believe that the Bible gives the body primacy. It is (we will argue in chapter III of this booklet) the anatomy of a person that reveals his or her gender calling. But under the influence of Cartesian mind-body dualism, contemporary culture has accepted the transgender argument that one's inner perception of gender is to be determined distinctly from anatomy, and even given primacy in decisions to reconcile the body to one's perceived gender. We believe these notions fundamental to the transgender movement rest upon erroneous approaches to mind-body dualism.

Descartes's name has become identified with such approaches that give the mind a distinct identity from, and primacy over, the body. Nevertheless, this notion can be traced farther back into older Hellenistic and Gnostic influences. In certain strands of classical Greek philosophy (such as Stoicism), the body was said to be "the alien garb of flesh" for the soul, an impediment to the soul, and a prison from which the soul seeks its release.[37] Gnostic teachings in the Greco-Roman world likewise promoted the superiority of the soul as the seat of the true self and the body as a foreign (or less important) element.[38] Scripture affirms the dual nature of humankind as, on the one hand, mind/soul/spirit and, on the other, flesh/body.[39] However, we believe it to be unbiblical to regard a person's soul as being the source of one's identity distinct from, or superior to, that of the body.

The Apostle Paul is particularly known for his employment of spirit-flesh contrasts in his epistles. And sadly, "Stoic-Gnostic-Cartesian"[40] assumptions about mind-body dualism have often been misread into the Apostle Paul. However, Paul uses the language of "spirit-flesh opposition" to distinguish between the realm of human existence (the "flesh") and that of human relationship to God's Spirit (the "spirit"), and to subject the former to the latter. He does not teach that the body is inferior to, or less essential to personal identity than the soul.[41] For example, Paul writes in Romans 8:5, "Those who live according to the flesh set their minds on the things of the flesh, but those who live according to the Spirit set their minds on the things of the Spirit." Some translations (like the ESV) capitalize the word "Spirit," since it is responsiveness to God's Spirit that Paul is contrasting with responsiveness to the world. Even if one regards Paul's words as referring to the person's own spirit, the point Paul is making is one of relationship to God's (disembodied) rule rather than submitting to the (embodied) temptations of the world. Paul himself makes this implication clear a few verses later, when he writes, "the mind that is set on the flesh is hostile to God, for it does not submit to God's law" (v. 7). Paul is not separating the mind and the body in a Cartesian distinction, but he is exhorting Christians to live—mind and body alike—in submission to God's law rather than human ideals (the "flesh").

Furthermore, Paul uses the language of the body to refer to the sensual nature of man (pictured in the physical senses) over against submission from the heart and mind to God. It is the bodily senses—touch, taste, smell, and seeing especially—that Paul frequently identifies as portals of temptation. He uses the language of the "fleshly" nature of man to capture that reality. Nevertheless, Paul is fully aware that many temptations emerge from within the mind of man independent of external sensory impulses (e.g., Rom. 1:21, 28). Paul's use of the language of the "flesh" as a source of temptation is one of idiom, rather than literally disdaining the body as the seat of sin over against a "pure" mind (as would, in fact, be asserted by his Stoic contemporaries). Paul affirms that the resurrection of the flesh is the pinnacle of Christian hope (e.g., 1 Cor. 15:50–57). Honoring the body as a part of the true self (not a disposable or secondary shell) in anticipation of its resurrection holiness is the present calling of the Christian (e.g., Rom. 6:11–14).

Sadly, Paul's language of spirit/flesh opposition has sometimes been misread as condoning a "Stoic-Gnostic-Cartesian" view of the soul as the true seat of personal identity in distinction from the body. However, this is not what Paul (or the rest of Scripture) teaches. A biblical view of the human person "does not justify us in saying that…the flesh or the body is a prison for the human soul."[42] The Scriptures (including Paul's epistles) have a high view of the body as essential to the person's self. Furthermore, when it comes to human gender, the body is not merely a vehicle for the soul's gender identity. We believe it is the body that indicates the person's God-given gender calling.

Influenced by Cartesian mind-body dualism, many in the transgender movement believe that a perceived contradiction between anatomical sex and one's inner self-perception is to be resolved by giving precedence to the psyche.[43] We do not deny that such experiences of contradiction exist and can be vexing. But we deny the assumption that the correct way to resolve the resulting questions about identity is by downplaying the witness of the anatomy in favor of neurological characteristics.

III

The Theology of Sex as Gender, and Gender as Calling

The transgender movement asserts a sharp distinction between anatomical sex and psychological/social gender. We recognize these two frontiers of male/female experience, but we deny that the two may be separated. Biblically, a person's social gender is identified by his or her anatomical sex. Humans are created by God with one or the other anatomical sex, and that sexual identity marks the person's gender calling. (Questions about ambiguous anatomy will be explored in chapter IV.) An individual may experience a vast array of traits and psychological inclinations which are atypical to *society's* expectations for the associated gender. However, social assumptions about what is typical for a given gender are not authoritative. It is a mark of God's goodness that he grants to men and women, traits and qualities in a variety of combinations, some more "typical" and some "atypical." We believe that persons are called by God to serve according to the gender indicated by the individual's anatomical sex.

Every person's experience of gender has been complicated, to varying degrees, by the fall. Since Adam's sin, humankind was "wholly defiled in all the faculties and parts of soul and body" (*Westminster Confession of Faith* [WCF] 6.2). Consequently, moral corruptions (which are sinful) as well as physical deformities (which are not sinful, but are disordered) have multiplied in variety and extent throughout the human race. This includes instances of either moral or biological confusion (or both) impacting either gender or sex (or both). However, our identity is not defined by our fallen condition. The Apostle Paul exhorts, "If we have been united with him in a death like his, we shall certainly be united with him in a resurrection like his....Present yourselves to God as those who have been brought from death to life..." (Rom. 6:5, 13). The focus of Paul's exhortation is to turn away from sin as those already living from our resurrected holiness. We believe it is consistent with Paul's thought similarly to live—as God gives us understanding and grace—from the gendered wholeness to which we are called now, and which we will experience in wholeness in the resurrection. How are we to discern our gender calling in cases where there is confusion?

The Bible recognizes that gender is both an anatomical identity and a social calling. In fact, biblical Hebrew uses different terms to emphasize anatomical sex and social gender. The Hebrew couplet *zakar* (male) and *neqebah* (female) refer particularly to anatomical manhood or womanhood, while the terms *'ish* (man) and *'ishah* (woman) are typically used with reference to social roles of manhood or womanhood.[44] Biblical Israel recognized that manhood and womanhood have both physical and social aspects. However, while Scripture recognizes these aspects of human gender, the coordinate biological and social identities are always aligned. A physical male (*zakar*) is consistently identified as a social man (*'ish*) in Scripture, and likewise a biological female (*neqebah*) as a social woman (*'ishah*). Nowhere do we find Scripture identifying a physical male (*zakar*) as socially female (*'ishah*), or vice versa.[45] The physical sex and social gender of the person are consistently united.[46]

Furthermore, the Bible maintains this connection of physical sex and social gender alongside its explicit awareness of the anatomically ambiguous. The Scriptures do not ignore the reality of anatomical ambiguity among some persons. Employing the term "eunuch" (Heb., *saris*, Gk., *eunouchos*), cases of anatomical ambiguity are recognized many times throughout Scripture, and are treated with grace and respect but never as requiring a change to unified, binary categories of male/female.

In certain societies contemporary with biblical Israel, some persons were "made eunuchs" by deliberate castration, typically for religious or political purposes. However, there are also those "who have been so from birth" (Matt. 19:12). The former practice (i.e., artificially making one a eunuch) is condemned among God's people (Deut. 23:1).[47] However, the latter (i.e., being born a eunuch) is also recognized among God's people in the Bible.

In New Testament times, Roman society used the term "eunuchs by nature" (*natura spadones*) for those born with sexual ambiguity.[48] Jews in that era used the term "eunuchs of the sun" (*saris khammah*) since "they were discovered to be eunuchs at the moment the sun shone upon them."[49] Jesus called them, "eunuchs who have been so from birth" (Matt. 19:12).[50] Some theologians suspect that the term "barren women" may also be used broadly enough in Scripture to include sexually ambiguous women.[51] In other words, Jesus and the biblical authors recognized the reality of sexually ambiguous persons, but we never find them being assigned to a third gender. A "eunuch" was always a man (or boy), and a "barren woman" was always a woman (or a girl). Jesus did not relegate the sexually ambiguous to a third gender.

In fact, at an earlier point in the same discussion in which Jesus speaks of "eunuchs," he specifically affirms the abiding binary categories of human callings:[52] "Have you not read that he who created them from the beginning made them male and female.... There are eunuchs who have been so from birth, and there are eunuchs who have been made eunuchs by men, and there are eunuchs who have made themselves eunuchs for the sake of the kingdom of heaven ..." (Matt. 19:4–12). These words from Jesus show us at least three important points: first, God created humankind in two categories, male and female; second, ambiguous experiences exist, but do not require additional categories beyond male and female; and third, those whose sexual identity is unclear are not to be devalued or made to feel less worthy as a consequence. In fact, in Jesus' words, there are some life callings which the "eunuch" is better suited to pursue than others. Jesus exalts the eunuch as a role model in this regard: "...and there are eunuchs who have made themselves eunuchs [i.e., who follow the eunuch's example of devotion][53] for the sake of the kingdom of heaven. Let the one who is able to receive this receive it" (Matt. 19:12).

Because contemporary culture holds that "existence precedes essence" (existentialism), the existence of intersex persons (e.g., those born eunuchs) is thought to require the introduction of a new category to account for them. Instead, Scripture teaches us to uphold the essence of human nature as gendered male or female with physical sex identical to the person's social gender. Nevertheless, Scripture also teaches us to recognize the reality of instances where making a determination may be unclear (or even impossible to make with certainty), and which must therefore be approached with respect and care.

Augustine tells us that intersex persons in the church of his day, whose proper gender could not be determined, were given "the benefit of the doubt" when identifying their gender. He writes, "Although androgynes, whom men also call hermaphrodites, are very rare, yet it is difficult to find periods when they do not occur. In them the marks of both sexes appear together in such a way that it is uncertain from which they should properly receive their name. However, our established manner of speaking has given them the gender of the better sex, calling them masculine."[54] While Augustine's description of the man as "the better sex" might be disturbing, his basic point to give every social advantage possible to such difficult cases ought to be appreciated as in keeping with the spirit of respect for the anatomically ambiguous taught by Christ. We ought not deny the reality of ambiguous and difficult cases of gender; nevertheless, the consistent calling of God's Word is to develop one's calling as male or female as anatomically revealed.

The Bible's foundational statement on human gender is provided in Genesis 1:26–28:[55] "Then God said, 'Let us make man in our image, after our likeness. And let them have dominion over the fish of the sea and over the birds of the heavens and over the livestock and over all the earth and over every creeping thing that creeps on the earth.' So God created man in his own image, in the image of God he created him; male and female he created them. And God blessed them. And God said to them, 'Be fruitful and multiply and fill the earth and subdue it and have dominion over the fish of the sea and over the birds of the heavens and over every living thing that moves on the earth.'"

There are three observations we will note from this passage. First, this passage introduces God's design for humankind as "male" and "female." These two categories are presented as normative categories into which all humans are ordered. This is not merely a description of the first humans as being a male and a female, with the possibility of other genders emerging later. Nor is it a description of these as the most common categories, with other genders being less common but also present within God's design. Genesis introduces the creation of humanity with these two gender categories as normative: male and female.

This traditional (and we believe correct) understanding of the text has been challenged. For example, Roy Ciampa has argued, "Genesis 1 offers us broad categories of difference: dry land and seas (v. 10); 'vegetation: seed-bearing plants and trees on the land that bear fruit with seed in it' (v. 11 NIV); sun, moon, and stars (v. 16); creatures that live on the ground (vv. 24–27). [But] this chapter does not list other forms or mixed forms regularly seen in creation: rivers, asteroids, planets, amphibians, dusk, dawn, etc."[56] By implication, then, Ciampa proposes that other variations of gender might be expected beyond the two named at creation. The analogy does not hold, however.

The other creation acts in Genesis 1 are described, and do allow for variations as Ciampa observes. The creation of Land and Sea does not negate the divine intention for "rivers" in the world (e.g., Gen. 2:10–14), nor does the creation of sea creatures and beasts of the earth deny the goodness of amphibians (e.g., frogs in Ex. 8:2). Nevertheless, the creation of humankind is uniquely presented within the creation narrative in the form of a prescriptive command. Humans are created as "male and female" as part of the command to steward the world as societies built around male and female membered families.[57] Thus binary genders are prescriptive, not merely descriptive.

The rest of Scripture confirms this interpretation. There are, as Ciampa observes, biblical affirmations of other mixed types developing from the creational descriptions, like rivers and amphibians and twilight and so forth. However, the consistent testimony of Scripture is that the creation categories "male and female" are normative. Throughout the rest of the Bible, humans are called to serve as men and women, even where ambiguous cases (eunuchs) do emerge as noted earlier. Genesis 1:26–28 identifies the two genders, "male and female," as God's design for humankind.

Second, we further observe that Genesis 1:26–28 conflates both the reproductive and the social duties of men and women within the same presentation of gender. This passage does not differentiate sexual roles from social roles. Instead, the same calling as male or female is here identified with both anatomical, reproductive roles ("be fruitful and multiply") as well as gendered, social roles ("Let them have dominion....Subdue it and have dominion...").[58] This passage is often called the "creation mandate" by theologians, because it contains the foundational mandate to develop both families and societies. We note that both of these roles—reproductive and the social stewardship roles—are conflated under the same binary designations: "male and female." To be sexually male is also to be socially male, and likewise for the female. The fact that the rest of the Bible's legal, historical, prophetic, and wisdom literature continues to reflect the unity of anatomical and social callings supports this conclusion.

This leads to a third observation. It is significant that Genesis 1:26–28 appoints the binary categories male and female using the *anatomical* (rather than social) terms of gender: "male (*zakar*) and female (*neqebah*) he created them" (v. 27). We believe this is done because it is the *anatomical* sex of the individual which indicates his or her gender calling. The social role of manhood (Heb., *'ish*) or womanhood (Heb., *'ishah*) is determined by the person's anatomical sex.

In fact, the Creation account reports that God created the first couple as anatomical man (*zakar*) and anatomical woman (*neqebah*). Then, based on these physical constitutions, the man and the woman recognize each other as *socially* gendered male and female: "Then the man said, 'This at last is bone of my bones and flesh of my flesh; she shall be called Woman (*'ishah*), because she was taken out of Man (*'ish*)'" (Gen. 2:23). It was the anatomical distinction of the man and the woman which led to their further attribution as *socially* male (*'ish*) and female (*'ishah*). Anatomical sex and social gender are kept in unity in the biblical view of humanity, with one's anatomical sex as the marker whereby one's gender calling is recognized.

This is not just a coincidence of language in the Genesis creation account. Throughout the rest of Scripture we find a consistent record of children identified at birth (i.e., by anatomy) as being male or female, who then grow up to fulfill the associated social, gender role (e.g., Gen. 29:31–30:24). As noted earlier, the Scriptures acknowledge the reality of intersex persons (e.g., "eunuchs from birth"), but these ambiguities are only identified with anatomical ambiguity and never with atypical psychological inclinations. Where there are social or personality traits that are atypical for a given gender, the Bible regards those traits as attributes to develop within one's anatomical gender rather than as a mismatch of anatomy and psychology.[59]

For example, Genesis reports typically masculine and typically feminine traits, respectively experienced by the twin boys of Isaac and Rebekah: "When [Rebekah's] days to give birth were completed, behold, there were twins in her womb. The first came out … [whom] they called Esau. Afterward his brother came out … [who] was called Jacob.…When the boys grew up, Esau was a skillful hunter, a man of the field, while Jacob was a quiet man, dwelling in tents. Isaac loved Esau because he ate of his game, but Rebekah loved Jacob" (Gen. 25:24–28). Jacob's traits were more naturally aligned with those of his mother than his father, not only in terms of his psychology ("a quiet man, dwelling in tents") but even in certain physiological features (he was smooth skinned; Gen. 27:11). "Notwithstanding Jacob's smooth [skin] and domestic traits, Scripture never so much as hints of any reason to regard Jacob [i.e., his psychological gender] as in anyway 'not conforming' to his [biological sex]."[60]

There are certain traits which are more commonly found among women than among men, and there may even be a neurological basis for the typical distribution of these traits. As some studies seem to suggest, the exposure of a developing child to higher testosterone levels during the first two months of pregnancy contributes to the development of male genitals; and if those high testosterone levels are still present in the latter half of the pregnancy, certain neurological features generally associated with a male psychology also develop. The full implication of these observations remains unclear, and the resulting Brain-Sex Theory is still hypothetical.[61] Nevertheless, if it is correct that the same hormone that serves a crucial role in the development of genitalia (testosterone) also contributes to certain neurological features later in development, this simply explains why certain neurological traits are typically associated with males. Just because testosterone is a factor in the development of male genitalia, does not mean that *everything* in which testosterone has a role is definitively masculine. Indeed, testosterone is not an exclusively male hormone, but is produced in a woman's ovaries as well, although typically at much lower levels than in most men.[62] To offer an admittedly simplistic, but, we hope, helpful illustration: Silicon Valley bears that name because of the important role that the element silicon serves in the production of modern electronics. However, not everything in which silicon serves an important role is an electronic device. Silicon is also used in the production of certain glues, it has become a useful material in mechanical devices such as watches,[63] and it may play a more important role in many biological processes than commonly appreciated.[64] As silicon is commonly identified with electronics but is not exclusively consigned to use in electronics, in a roughly analogous manner testosterone is popularly viewed as a "masculine hormone" since it does play an important role in the male anatomy. However, not everything in which testosterone plays a role (including its role in brain development) is thereby definitively masculine.

Even if scientific research further demonstrates that certain psychological traits more typical among males are indeed linked to high testosterone levels during fetal brain development, we recognize this explains why those traits are more commonly experienced by men. But we are not persuaded this justifies placing the stigma of gender mismatch upon that boy whose *in utero* brain development occurred with lower than typical testosterone levels. A person born with a male anatomy but whose brain development *in utero* may have experienced less testosterone exposure is still fully and wholly masculine. It is an error of culture that certain personality traits are labeled as "masculine" or "feminine." Perhaps it is God's desire that most men would have certain personality traits, so he ordained that the same hormone behind male genital development would also contribute toward certain neurological features. However, there may also be wise and good reasons why God, in his providence, would appoint that some boys develop atypical neurological characteristics from different hormonal activity *in utero*—but who are still fully male socially as well as anatomically. The science remains speculative and uncertain; nevertheless, if the postulated hormone mechanics behind Brain-Sex Theory prove true, the assertion that brains are "gendered" does not follow.

Society needs men and women who (like the biblical patriarch, Jacob) possess personality traits that break with gender stereotypes. Stanton Jones points to biblical examples: "We have positive precedents in biblical stories of women who were prophetesses, judges, or who participated in acts of war,"[65] roles which required traits Old Testament society would typically have associated with men. A woman with a feminine anatomy and yet psychological traits and interests more commonly experienced by men is still as much a woman as more stereotypical women—regardless of the way hormones (or chromosomes) contribute to that development.

Modern science has only begun to scratch the surface in its efforts to describe a biological basis for gender, and it would not be surprising if some form of Brain-Sex Theory is confirmed with individuals whose neurological development does not match the norm for their anatomical sex. However, such a mismatch would be a result of the fall. While such an experience would have real complications requiring unusual grace to overcome, we do not believe that embracing a "third gender" or "mixed gender" identity is in keeping with God's calling. In a sense, it might be an accurate description of a person's experience, but it is never an accurate description of the person's identity and calling before God. As with any disorder of the body, it is not that disorder (even if at the level of neurology) that defines a person but rather the ideal to which we are called in resurrection hope. We therefore urge all persons to discern their gender calling, namely as male or as female, to exercise faithfully before God and before one another. Where there is confusion regarding one's gender calling, it is the sexual anatomy that is to be given priority as the marker of that calling. While the contemporary influence of a Cartesian mind-body dualism inclines many in our society to grant preference to the soul (or to neurological characteristics) where there is confusion, we believe the light of Scripture leads us to honor the body as the marker of one's sex and gender calling. And we want to stress, *gender is a calling.* It is often a hard calling, not only for those who experience gender dysphoria, but even many with a straightforward cisgendered experience often struggle to be faithful to that gender calling. Christians ought to be sensitive to the varied challenges we face in our various struggles to walk out our manifold callings—gender being just one aspect thereof.

The Scriptures are full of examples of men and women with a wide array of emotional and psychological traits, but never with gender roles distinct from their anatomical sex. It is our conviction that human gender is anatomically indicated, and despite a wide (and beautiful) variety of traits among men and women, social gender roles are always to comport with one's anatomical sex. It is important to recognize that gender is a *calling* to be fulfilled, not simply an identity one discovers. To put it simply, a person's *sexual identity* (anatomy) reveals his or her *gender calling* (social role).[66]

IV

Anatomical Ambiguity (Intersex)

Normally, a baby's anatomy at birth makes his or her sexuality evident. Furthermore, that child's physical changes through life (especially during puberty) normally follow a typical course associated with male or female sexual development. However, there are rare but important instances where a baby is born with ambiguous anatomical features, making sex and gender identification difficult, or whose physical development does not follow typical paths. The terms *hermaphrodism*, *intersex*, or *Disorders of Sex Development* (DSD) are used for such cases.

According to the "Consensus Statement on Management of Intersex Disorders" (produced in 2006 by an international team of experts on intersex conditions), roughly one in 4,500 live births bring a child into the world with ambiguous genitalia.[67] Sadly, there has often been a tendency to regard such conditions as "freaks of nature"[68] leading to shame. In reaction to that tendency, some advocates have sought to promote recognition of a third (or more) gender(s) in order to uphold the dignity and honor of the small but significance percentage of the population born intersex.[69] We believe it is essential for the church to affirm the dignity of intersex individuals as persons made in the image of God, regardless of the presence of physical anomalies of this or any other kind. However, we do not believe it is necessary to create a new sex/gender category to do so. Ironically, to suggest that the recognition of "intersex" as a third gender is necessary to affirm the individual's human dignity would be to suggest that a person's sexuality is central to the divine likeness. We affirm that humans are called to reflect God's image in their roles as men or women; but we deny that the quality of a person's participation in the divine image is dependent on physical characteristics of any kind. Intersex individuals are fully human bearers of the divine image. Furthermore, intersex persons are fundamentally male or female, even if anatomical disorders make it difficult to identify their gender calling—and in some very rare cases, impossible to determine with certainty.

Child development expert Leonard Sax has argued (from a strictly scientific perspective), "The available data support the conclusion that human sexuality is a dichotomy, not a continuum. More than 99.98% of humans are either male or female. If the term *intersex* is to retain any clinical meaning, the use of this term should be restricted to those conditions in which chromosomal sex is inconsistent with phenotypic [i.e., anatomical] sex, or in which the phenotype is not classifiable as either male or female…occurring in fewer than 2 out of every 10,000 births."[70] We concur that there are two genders, with the added conviction that God created humans with a gender calling indicated in their anatomy.

There are a number of known medical conditions which can lead to sexual ambiguity.[71] For example, *Androgen Insensitivity Syndrome* (AIS) is a condition where a child is born with the typically male XY chromosomes and the internal organs of a male. However, due to an inability to respond to testosterone, the developing child does not develop male genitalia. Thus having the external appearance of a girl at birth, it is often not until puberty when a failure to menstruate leads to further examination, revealing the presence of undescended testicles internally and the absence of female reproductive organs. An AIS child raised as a girl may suddenly be found, in fact, to be a boy. We note that this determination is still based on anatomy, although it is the internal reproductive system which confirms that a brith defect led to misleading external features. In another, comparable disorder called *Congenital Adrenal Hyperplasia* (CAH), an infant with typically female XX chromosomes is exposed to an excess of androgen *in utero*. When born, the child's genitalia may be either ambiguous or with proportions that give the appearance of a boy, even though internal reproductive organs are female. As in the case of AIS, a child born with CAH may be raised as a boy until her true anatomical gender as female is discovered due to bodily changes later in development.

Once again, the basis of sexual and gender determination in these cases is still anatomical, although the CAH girl's external traits may disguise the presence of her otherwise female anatomy. Various other conditions can similarly contribute to mistaken classifications at birth, or even to lifelong ambiguity. In some extremely rare cases, the anatomical features may be so profoundly ambiguous as to make certainty impossible.

In such circumstances, the individual should be affirmed as a person with dignity made in the image of God. Where anatomical gender can be discerned (often through examination of the internal reproductive organs),[72] the malformed features should in no wise be regarded as lessening his or her full masculinity or femininity. Where anatomical gender is impossible to determine, the church ought to fully support and respect the best efforts of the individual (with support from family and medical professionals) to adopt the gender calling that seems correct. While we reject the presupposition of Augustine that the male gender is "better,"[73] we concur with the spirit of the Early Church's respect for truly ambiguous individuals making the best judgment possible.

Furthermore, where physiological conditions have hindered proper development and surgical procedures are available that legitimately support the individual's anatomical gender, such procedures *may* be prudent. However, many persons born with intersex conditions regret that well-intentioned parents and doctors made too hasty a determination to perform surgery in infancy that is later found to have been mistaken.[74] Surgical procedures in such circumstances may be appropriate, but require great care, much medical counsel, and prayer. In those instances where a wrong sex/gender identification is made in infancy, and the proper anatomical sex/gender comes to light in later years, a decision regarding "gender transition" ought to be fully and lovingly supported by the church.

We deny the rightness of gender transitions based on psychological, neurological, or social bases. Individuals whose psychological or social traits seem to align with the opposite sex ought to be encouraged and helped to embrace their calling to bring their atypical traits into their service as the gender indicated by their anatomical sex. However, since sexual anatomy is the right foundation for discerning one's gender calling, the church needs to support persons who "transition" after later anatomical findings reveal an earlier determination was, in fact, incorrect.

By respecting those conditions where surgical procedures and/or "gender transitions" may be theologically prudent, we affirm our core conviction that God has created humans as male or female, and that our gender calling is revealed in our anatomical sex. All persons struggle to discern aspects of their calling. For most people, discerning their gender is not one of those difficult aspects of calling to discern. But for some, anatomical ambiguity makes discerning their gender calling difficult. We call on the church to provide loving support and full acceptance of these individuals.

V

Conclusions and Pastoral Guidance

Over the past century in Western society, virtually every aspect of human sexuality has been loosed from its mooring in God's Word. No-fault divorce, sexual "freedom" and the aggressive promotion of contraception, the mainstreaming of pornography and explicit images in movies and advertising, the dehumanization of the unborn to justify abortion, the normalization of homosexuality, the legalization of same-sex marriage, and transgenderism are all various fronts of the same cultural fascination with "setting sexuality free" from its anchor in God's Word.

To make this point is not to suggest that all proponents of this ongoing "sexual revolution" are motivated by sexual lust. Many proponents of one or another of these movements are motivated by lust,[75] but not all. Some proponents of these movements are looking for healing and redemption in their struggle with sexual brokenness of various forms. It is important for Christians to recognize the difference, and to speak with prophetic boldness against the sin of lust while also ministering with hope and compassion to those bearing the burdens of brokenness. We must promote the hope of the gospel, including the gospel promise of complete physical and emotional wholeness in glory, and the real possibility of growth in that wholeness through the means of grace today. Those who lack that hope will seek to solve their sexual brokenness through other means.

Marriage conflicts are real and painful, but we reject the unbiblical (and socially destabilizing) "solution" promoted through no-fault divorce. An unexpected or unwanted pregnancy creates huge burdens for a young woman; but terminating the life forming within is a tragic "solution." Sexual temptation—whether same-sex oriented or heterosexually oriented—is a genuine affliction that requires God's redemption; granting a license to surrender to those lusts is not a true solution. Likewise, gender confusion requires biblical care to restore confidence and joy with the gender to which God has called each individual as indicated by his or her anatomy.

We believe that God created humankind, and the order he appointed to humankind is good (Gen. 1:26–31). To approach these many issues of sexual brokenness from the foundation provided in God's Word enables us to promote the fostering of an individual's humanity to its fullest design with the hope of present growth and eventually, in the resurrection, realized perfection.[76] We urge the church to persevere in her trust in God's design for humanity and human sexuality in all these frontiers, including gender and its many forms of this-worldly brokenness.

In this booklet we have endeavored to explore issues surrounding the transgender movement from just such a confidence in God's Word and his love. We believe it is important to promote the wholeness of those struggling with gender confusion by helping affirm them in their anatomical gender calling. We reject the false philosophies enumerated in this booklet and call for care to be pursued based on a biblical anthropology, including a biblical doctrine of gender. We believe the most realistic and meaningful help for "gender dysphoria" is that which is provided through a biblical understanding of sexuality and gender. God has appointed the binary sexes; and God has called us to serve in the gender that comports with our sexual anatomy, allowing for all the variety of our individual traits—as atypical as those traits may be—to play into that calling. We believe that special support must be shown toward those struggling to discern their gender calling due to sexual ambiguity, and that loving exhortation must be offered to those confused by non-stereotypical psychological traits to bring those traits into their unique fulfillment of the gender calling indicated in their birth anatomy.

Within these parameters established in this booklet, we offer the following points of guidance for pastors and Christians responding to these matters:

a. Listen in order to understand—It is a show of great trust if someone struggling with "gender dysphoria" opens up about that area of his or her life. Guard the confidence and respect of that trust, and exercise the wisdom of James: "be quick to hear, slow to speak" (Jas. 1:19). Rather then hastily offering counsel, it is first important to take time to hear and to understand the unique nature of this individual's experience. No two experiences are the same. A booklet like this one might chart out some general principles of theology, but discipleship is a work of ministry to the unique needs and opportunities of specific persons. Demonstrate patience to listen and to understand the particular experiences of the individual who opens his or her struggles to you.

b. Minister the gospel—The Apostle Paul suffered from an unnamed affliction, and he prayed repeatedly for deliverance, concluding, "Three times I pleaded with the Lord about this, that it should leave me. But he said to me, 'My grace is sufficient for you, for my power is made perfect in weakness.' Therefore I will boast all the more gladly of my weakness, so that the power of Christ may rest upon me. For the sake of Christ, then, I am content with weakness, insults, hardships, persecutions, and calamities. For when I am weak, then I am strong" (2 Cor. 12:8–10). In this passage, we are reminded that the gospel is not given as a "quick fix" for all our struggles. We do have the confidence of perfect healing—body and soul—in the final resurrection (1 Cor. 15:42–44). And we are encouraged to pray and to pursue healing and growth in the present, as God is pleased to grant it. (Paul did pray repeatedly[77] for his affliction!) However, the gospel ministers to us at a much more profound level than mere "fixes" for our struggles. The gospel points to the root cause of all human brokenness including gender dysphoria and bodily malformations (namely the human fall and original sin); the gospel points us to the solution for all sin, both original and actual (namely atonement and communion with God through Christ); the gospel assures us of full and final sanctification in the resurrection; and the gospel grants us hope and purpose to face our trials today with joy and victory—either through deliverance from them or, as in the case of Paul's affliction, by the Spirit's fellowship to bring us spiritual blessing through or in spite of them. It is important when ministering to those who struggle with any significant affliction or temptation, not to become fixated on just one area of struggle but to offer whole-gospel ministry to the whole person, centered in Christ as our Savior from sin and its curse. It must, furthermore, be remembered that Christians are vulnerable to the same temptations as non-believers. To be a Christian is not to be immune to certain kinds of temptation, but rather to have the Spirit's help to face them and the

Son's provision to atone for them (2 Cor. 10:13). Mark Yarhouse helpfully writes, "It should not be assumed that greater Christlikeness is the same as having gender dysphoria abate. Many people who know and love Christ have besetting conditions that have simply not resolved as a result of their belief in Christ as their savior. Indeed, it may very well be that it is in the context of these enduring conditions that God brings about greater Christlikeness."[78] Therefore, incorporate concern for gender confusion into a comprehensive ministry of the gospel for discipleship.

c. Cases of anatomical ambiguity—When churches come into contact with, or have within their membership, individuals with intersex conditions, it is important to affirm the dignity and image of God fully shared by them and to give every effort to ensure they are not made to feel inferior because of their condition. In fact, church leaders should be careful in their speech at all times to ensure those with physical defects of any type are not made to feel unwelcome in the church. Individuals who face the challenges of anatomical ambiguity will, for good reason, typically keep those details secret. Pastors and church leaders should address gender issues in a way that is sensitive, both as a model for all congregants and as a ministry of respect to those who may bear this particular burden.

In those rare instances where sexual ambiguity is profound, such that one's gender calling is not certain, that uncertainty is reason for prayer and support, not condemnation. Other individuals struggle to discern God's calling on them as discerned in other aspects of their unique constitution; those with profound sexual ambiguity are no different in principle, they simply have a greater struggle discerning their proper gender calling than most. It is important to support the intersex individual's efforts to determine, with competent medical counsel, their anatomical sex and its coordinate gender calling. In those rare cases where this may involve surgical procedures or even a gender transition (when the anatomy was mistaken in infancy and later correctly identified), the church should show full support and affirmation for the individual. There is enough emotional shame that surrounds these challenges; Christians ought to bend over backward to keep from adding to that sense of shame but instead to promote the dignity and honor of the person.

When counseling parents of a newborn whose anatomy is ambiguous, the same principles as above apply to the full support to be extended as the parents, in consultation with medical experts, seek to know the gender calling of their child. Although medical experts once promoted radical, corrective surgeries on infants, we are thankful that medical advice today cautions against irreversible surgical procedures on infants.[79] Even in those cases where intersex conditions exist, it would seem prudent to minimize surgical intervention to what actually promotes health. The role of medicine is to serve the ministry of redemption in the area of health, to the extent medically possible. It is not the role of medicine to provide the hope of transformation and recreation in the face of every defect; for that, we have the promise of resurrection.

d. Cases of perceived (psychological) transgender identity—A person who experiences a self-perceived bent toward identification with the opposite gender ought not feel ashamed at those inclinations, but should be encouraged to respond to those feelings biblically. The perception may be strong, and it may legitimately arise from brain biology that inclines a person toward psychological traits more commonly identified with the opposite gender. But one should not *interpret* that self-perception as indication of a mismatched "brain sex." Instead, he or she ought to embrace these providentially granted psychological traits with a commitment to exercise them within his or her anatomically indicated gender calling. "Feelings *do not define you.*>They may, at least partly, describe *how* you are, but they do not describe *who* you are."[80] The goal here is to minister affirmation of the person's wholeness as a man or a woman, a boy or a girl. It is the transgender movement that is telling people that "something is wrong with them" if their psychology does not "measure up" to what is normal for individuals with their anatomy. We want to affirm that such persons are free and right to embrace their wholeness as "cisgender" regardless of how normal or abnormal their psychological experience of their gender might be. "Where one might claim that there is a disconnect between self-consciousness and embodiment, the Christian must tenderly and compassionately advise that it is the mental—that is, the self-consciousness and sense of personal identity—that must be conformed to the body rather than the body conformed to the individual's mistaken self-perception."[81]

e. Cases of name and pronoun change—When an individual has already claimed a gender identity contrary to his or her birth anatomy, he or she will often assume a new name and a new set of preferred pronouns. Should a Christian address the person by his or her new or former name and pronouns? It is important to recognize this question, but to avoid a simplistic "one size fits all" answer. On the one hand, a Christian ought to establish respectful communication with others, addressing them in a manner that shows love for the person and avoids any tone of disdain. On the other hand, a Christian ought to guard against communicating support for another's ungodly decisions (but to do so without a "holier than thou" attitude, mindful that we all "fall short of the glory of God;" Rom. 3:23). A Christian should seek to address a self-presenting transgender individual within these parameters.

Unfortunately, those who adopt a new gender and a new name may interpret your response to their name-change as indicating both your acceptance or non-acceptance of their gender transition as well as your acceptance or non-acceptance of him or her as a person. Therefore, a transgender name and pronoun change often creates an unavoidable dilemma that cannot be resolved simply. In some cases, this may involve a conversation to express commitment to the person despite an inability to use particular pronouns. Conversely, a conversation may be required to express that your use of the person's new name is an expression of commitment to the person but not an endorsement of his or her gender transition. However one responds to a person's new name and pronoun preference, our goal must be to communicate respect for the person without giving a false witness regarding the abiding integrity of one's anatomically indicated birth gender.

f. Cases of gender transition, in a son or daughter—One of the greatest challenges of parenting is when adult children make decisions that grieve their parents. It will be difficult for parents when their adult children reject the faith in which they were raised, or when they make other significant choices contrary to the parents' convictions. One such circumstance is when adult (or soon-to-be-adult) children identify as transgender. Parents may feel pressed either to embrace the child's transgender decision as an expression of unconditional love for the child, or (on the other extreme) to renounce the child's decision in ways that essentially amount to rejecting the child. Neither of these extremes is necessary nor would either be proper. Parents can communicate their own biblical convictions on the matter, while also assuring the son or daughter of their continuing love. A "transgender" son or daughter who has come to believe their self-perceived gender is their real identity may endeavor to persuade parents that rejecting gender transition is equivalent to rejecting them. We should equip and support parents in responding to such pressure, to maintain that love for the individual does not necessitate approval of his or her "transition." In this situation, such parents join the long list of

Christian parents through the ages who have prayed for wandering sons and daughters, endeavoring to uphold a consistent witness with abiding love. Hopefully, God will be pleased also to add these parents to the long list of those who have rejoiced to see the Spirit renew a prodigal's heart and bring him or her to Christ and to his ways.

g. Cases of sex change—The proper purpose of medicine is to promote the wholeness of the body. It is tragic that the transgender movement has led to the promotion of surgeries that mutilate and damage otherwise healthy bodies. We recognize that, in a small number of cases where disorders have led to malformed anatomy, some surgical procedures may be appropriate. However, those are instances where surgery is undertaken to correct what is damaged, not to damage what is physically healthy. Where an irreversible sex change operation has already been done, the person's sex/gender is still the one with which they were born. The surgical procedure does not change the person's sex/gender calling, although it may move the person into the condition of "eunuchs who have been made eunuchs by men" (Matt. 19:12) in how they carry out their calling. An important point to underscore from that quotation from Jesus is that, even when a physically irreversible procedure has taken place, the value of the person and his or her usefulness to the Lord in service is not lost. Humble repentance and full forgiveness for further service ought to be the goal.[82]

h. Transgender marriage—With the legalization of homosexual marriage in America and the political recognition of gender transitions, the church is facing a new frontier of state legalized marriages that are lacking in moral foundations. As in the case of adulterous remarriages, Christians are in a place where it will become an increasing reality to interact with acquaintances as legally married partners when they present themselves as such in spite of an immoral foundation to that marriage. Nevertheless, Christian ministers ought never to knowingly solemnize an adulterous marriage, whatever the reason might be for its moral illegitimacy under the standards of Scripture. A homosexual marriage is immoral and ought not to be performed by a minister. A marriage between two transgender individuals would also be unbiblical, as God calls for a marriage to be established on the basis of a man fulfilling the gender of his birth anatomy and undertaking the duties of a husband (and father) and a woman taking the duties of a wife (and mother). We believe that Christian ministers must not solemnize these marriages.

i. Cases of atypical gender traits—Gender is anatomically (not socially) defined; nevertheless, personality traits are not anatomically fixed but are, indeed, socially typified. The church should resist our culture's tendency to fuel discomfort with one's anatomically indicated gender because of gender non-typical personality traits. God takes delight in variety and in the unexpected. Certain kinds of traits and interests may be typical for men and boys, while other inclinations are usual for women and girls; but it is vital for Christians to distinguish between what is normal and what is normative. Personality traits and psychological inclinations must not be treated as gender normative. In this age when the culture wrongly ascribes normative authority to one's inner inclinations, it is increasingly important for the church to affirm and fully accept, without any teasing or belittling, those youth and adults in our midst whose traits are atypical for their gender.

j. Cases of gender discomfort—God's calling upon a person is not always easy. Some persons wish they could become athletes, but God has not gifted them with the traits for athletic accomplishment. Others long to be musicians but lack an ear for music. There are many ways in which our God-given traits do not always match our present desires. Gender is also a category of God's calling upon a person. Encourage the individual to recognize their gender as a calling to accept out of trust in God's love. But do not approach the conversation as though such a change of heart is a simple matter. A Christian friend should demonstrate appreciation for the weightiness of this calling to contentment—and one day, we hope, to happiness—with their God-given gender.[83] When a person's gender desires do not match their anatomy, neither changing the anatomy nor a change of heart will be easy. The reason for accepting the witness of anatomy and seeking the Spirit's help with a change of heart is not because it is the supposedly "easier" option; this is the direction to pursue because it is the path of faith, trusting in God's wisdom and grace.

k. Guard against politicized morality—One of the unfortunate features of American "evangelicalism" has been its politicization. The calling of the church is to minister the whole gospel of Jesus Christ to the world. Unfortunately, it has become popular in American Christianity to separate Christian atonement from Christian morality, and to promote the atonement inside the church while promoting "Judeo-Christian values" through political means. The very idea that values can be at the same time both affirmative of Judaism (i.e., rejecting Christ) and Christianity (i.e., embracing Christ) is to overlook how central the atonement is to any hope of moral reform. Issues like abortion, homosexuality, and transgenderism are important frontiers for ministering the whole gospel—that is, a *cross-centered* call to holiness. Voting for morally upright politics is certainly good, but we must guard against getting caught up in the popular "evangelical" enthusiasm for politicized morality. Christians should be careful not to support every anti-transgender effort, especially those filled with condemnation and politics but lacking in cross-centered grace. We must be careful our moral witness is truly a witness of God's grace to confront and forgive sinners.

l. Expect children to wonder about gender—Child development experts note that it is common for children to go through stages of wondering about their gender, and even to wish they were the other gender, or to show interest in the clothing (or jewelry) of the other sex. Typically, by the time a child reaches adolescence, those curiosities dissipate. In the present culture, it is easy to over-react to the common "cross-gender" curiosities of growing children. Certainly, Christian parents should be alert for abnormal levels of gender discomfort in a child which might require special prayer, counsel, or support. But we also must ensure that the prominence of transgender issues in the culture does not lead us to overinterpret normal questions among children.

*   *   *

These points of guidance are by no means comprehensive. But we hope they provide some help for pastors, elders, and other church members thinking about these issues of gender and transgenderism. As the transgender movement continues to advance rapidly in our culture, it is important for the church to be well-equipped to minister and to live out a biblical vision for sexuality and gender with the love of Christ.

Endnotes

1. *The Gospel & Sexual Orientation* (M. LeFebvre, ed.; Pittsburgh: Crown & Covenant, 2012), 5–8; M. LeFebvre, "Homosexuality in America: Retrospect & Prospect as Covenanters," *Reformed Presbyterian Theological Journal* 2.2 (2016), 21–7.

2. Kevin D. Williamson, "The Transgender Culture War: Accommodation Will Never Be Enough," *National Review* 68.10 (June 13, 2016), 30.

3. These definitions are adapted primarily from Mark A. Yarhouse, *Understanding Gender Dysphoria: Navigating Transgender Issues in a Changing Culture* (Downers Grove: InterVarsity Press, 2015), 17–19. For a more extensive glossary of relevant terms, see Yarhouse, *Gender Dysphoria*, 20–21.

4. Both men and women possess all of these hormones, but the levels of androgen are typically higher in males than in females and vice versa with estrogen and progesterone. (See pp. 27–28.)

5. John R. Blosnich, et al, "Prevalence of Gender Identity Disorder and Suicide Risk Among Transgender Veterans Utilizing Veterans Health Administration Care," *American Journal of Public Health* 103.1 (2013), e28. These statistics are based primarily on studies conducted in Belgium and the Netherlands. Researchers admit, however, that confident numbers are difficult to ascertain. One survey of various measurements notes, "Prevalence estimates range from 1:10,000 to 1:100,000 for MF [i.e., male to female transition] and 1:30,000 to 1:400,000 for FM [i.e., female to male transition]." (Cindy Meston and Penny Frohlich, "The Psychobiology of Sexual and Gender Identity Disorders," in *Biological Psychiatry* [H. D'Haenen, et al, eds.; John Wiley & Sons, Ltd: Chichester, UK, 2002], 1110.) The *DSM-5* gives the following prevalence for "gender dysphoria": "For natal adult males, prevalence ranges from 0.005% to 0.014%, and for natal females, from 0.002% to 0.003%." (*DSM-5*, 454.) Cf., Lindsay Collin, "Prevalence

of Transgender Depends on the 'Case' Definition: A Systematic Review," *The Journal of Sexual Medicine* 13.4 (2016), 613–26.

6. *Diagnostic and Statistical Manual of Mental Disorders: DSM-IV-TR* (Washington, D.C.: American Psychiatric Association, 2000), 576–82.

7. *Diagnostic and Statistical Manual of Mental Disorders: DSM-5* (Washington, D.C.: American Psychiatric Association, 2013), 452.

8. "Gender Dysphoria [Fact Sheet]" (American Psychiatric Association, 2013), 1.

9. "Gender Dysphoria," 1–2.

10. The *DSM-5* currently recognizes "anxiety and depressive disorders" among those commonly comorbid with gender dysphoria. (DSM-5, 458–9.)

11. Oliver O'Donovan, "Transsexualism and Christian Marriage," *The Journal of Religious Ethics* 11.1 (1983), 136–7.

12. Paul R. McHugh, "Surgical Sex," *First Things* 147 (2004), 35.

13. Paul R. McHugh, "Transgender Surgery Isn't the Solution: A Drastic Physical Change Doesn't Address Underlying Psycho-Social Troubles," *The Wall Street Journal*, June 12, 2014; also as interviewed in Perry Chiaramonte, "Controversial Therapy for Pre-Teen Transgender Patient Raises Questions" (Oct. 17, 2011), online at: www.foxnews.com/us/2011/10/17/controversial-therapy-for-young-transgender-patients-raises-questions.html (accessed Feb. 2017).

14. E.g., Jochen Hess, et al, "Satisfaction with Male-to-Female Gender Reassignment Surgery: Results of a Retrospective Analysis," *Deutsches Ärzteblatt International* 111 (2014), 795–801; Audrey Gorin-Lazard, et al, "Hormonal Therapy is Associated with Better Self-Esteem, Mood, and Quality of Life in Transsexuals," *Journal of Nervous and Mental Disease* 201.11 (2013), 996–1000; Yolanda Smith, et al, "Sex Reassignment: Outcomes and Predictors of Treatment for Adolescent and Adult Transsexuals," *Psychological Medicine* 35 (2005), 89–99.

15. "After SRS, the transsexual person's expectations were met at an emotional and social level, but less so at the physical and sexual level." (Griet De Cuypere, et al, "Sexual and Physical Health After Sex Reassignment Surgery," *Archives of Sexual Behavior* 34.6 [2005], 679–90.)

16. DSD is also sometimes defined as "Disorders of Sex Differentiation" or "Differences of Sex Development."

17. Silvan Agius, "Human Rights and Intersex People: Issue Paper" (Office of the Commissioner for Human Rights, Council of Europe, Issues Paper; Strasbourg Cedex, France: Council of Europe, 2015), 22–3.

18. Dick F. Swaab and Alicia Garcia-Falgueras, "Sexual Differentiation of the Human Brain in Relation to Gender Identity and Sexual Orientation," *Functional Neurology* 24.1 (2009), 17. Cf., Jan Wacker, et al, "Prenatal Testosterone and Personality: Increasing the Specificity of Trait Assessment to Detect Consistent Associations with Digit Ration (2D:4D)," *Journal of Research in Personality* 47 (2013), 171–7.

19. One important contraindication may be found in studies of women diagnosed with Congenital Adrenal Hyperplasia (CAH), a condition which involves an

overproduction of testosterone *in utero*. Although CAH is known to cause ambiguous genitalia, gender dysphoria is not typical among girls/women with CAH. (Meston and Frohlich, "Psychobiology of Gender Identity Disorders," 1110.) However, some recent studies question these findings. (Celina Cohen-Bendahan, et al, "Prenatal Sex Hormone Effects on Child & Adult Sex-Typed Behavior: Methods & Findings," *Neuroscience and Biobehavioral Reviews* 29.2 [2005], 353–84; Heino Meyer-Bahlburg, "Gender and Sexuality in Classic Congenital Adrenal Hyperplasia," *Endocrinology & Metabolism Clinics of North America* 30.1 [2001], 155–71.)

20. Jiang-Ning Zhou, et al, "A Sex Difference in the Human Brain and its Relation to Transsexuality," Nature 378 (1995), 68.

21. Yarhouse, *Gender Dysphoria*, 69.

22. See Yarhouse, *Gender Dysphoria*, 67–83.

23. Alice Domurat Dreger, *Hermaphrodites and the Medical Invention of Sex* (Cambridge, Mass.: Harvard University Press, 2001), 6. Cf., R. Albert Mohler, Jr., *We Cannot Be Silent: Speaking Truth to a Culture Redefining Sex, Marriage, and the Very Meaning of Right and Wrong* (Nashville, Tenn.: Nelson Books, 2015), 72–3.

24. For lists and usage examples of gender-neutral pronouns, see the "Gender Neutral Pronoun Blog" (genderneutralpronoun.wordpress.com).

25. Quoted in Cintra Wilson, "The Reluctant Transgender Role Model," *New York Times* (May 8, 2011), ST1. (Available online at www.nytimes.com/2011/05/08/fashion/08CHAZ.html.)

26. For a helpful glossary of these and other terms used in the transgender movement, see Yarhouse, *Gender Dysphoria*, 20–1.

27. Jean-Paul Sartre, *Existentialism Is a Humanism* (Carol Macomber, translator; New Haven, Connecticut: Yale University Press, 2007), 20.

28. Sartre, *Existentialism*, 20–21.

29. Sartre, *Existentialism*, 20–22.

30. Although full-blown existentialism is typically atheistic, the roots of existentialism emerged among Christian philosophers. Søren Kierkegaard is called the Father of Existentialism because he developed some of the seminal ideas of the movement. Kierkegaard's effort was to emphasize the importance of an authentic response to Christ over against a mere "categorical" Christianity. In this booklet, we are interacting with atheistic existentialism as the movement developed in later generations.

31. Crowell, Steven, "3.1 Anxiety, Nothingness, the Absurd" in "Existentialism," *The Stanford Encyclopedia of Philosophy* (Spring 2016 Edition), online at: plato.stanford.edu/archives/spr2016/entries/existentialism.

32. Mohler, *We Cannot Be Silent*, 71.

33. Dreger, *Hermaphrodites*, 8.

34. René Descartes, *The Philosophical Writings of Descartes* (trans. John Cottingham, et al; Cambridge: Cambridge University Press, 1984-1991), 3.208.

35. E.g., *WCF* 32.

36. Christopher West, *Fill These Hearts: God, Sex, and the Universal Longing* (New York: Image, 2012), 9.

37. Eduard Schweitzer, "σάρξ in the Greek World," *TDNT*, 7.103–4.

38. Kurt Rudolph, "Gnosticism," *ABD* 2.1033–40.

39. For the purposes of this booklet, we accept the traditional dichotomous view of humankind. However, we believe the basic thrust of our argument would also work within a trichotomous view and thus does not require a particular resolution of the classic dichotomy/trichotomy debate.

40. By stringing these terms together, we are not suggesting that these three philosophical trends are identical or even related. We simply seek to focus on the particular notion which has come into western cultural thought with reinforcement from each of these various philosophical systems: the notion that the self is identified with the soul in distinction from the body.

41. See esp., I. Howard Marshall, "Living in the 'Flesh'," *Bibliotheca Sacra* 159 (2002), 387–403.

42. Rudolf Meyer, "Flesh in Judaism," *TDNT* 7.114.

43. Typically, mind-body dualism (especially in its gnostic formulations) gives priority to the soul in a manner that despises or demeans the body. Remarkably, transgenderism gives priority to the soul for determining identity, but then goes to the other extreme to over-exalt the body. "Transsexuals do not retreat from their bodies into a Gnostic spirituality; if anything, they are preoccupied with them" (O'Donovan, "Transsexualism," 147). "We hardly despise the body. Indeed, transgenderism does not claim that the soul, a prisoner in the body, should seek to rid itself of physicality. Rather, in order for inner peace to be achieved, we must create the body we want" (Patrick Jones, Response to Robert P. George, "Gnostic Liberalism," *First Things* [Feb. 2017], online at: www.firstthings.com/article/2017/02/letters).

44. Victor P. Hamilton, "2351(זכר)," *NIDOTTE* 1.1107.

45. This might be contrasted with, for instance, the Egyptian example of Hatshepsut who reigned as queen of Egypt (depicted in female attire) for several years, but eventually adopted male titles and male attire (including the symbolic beard of a pharaoh), reigning thereafter as pharaoh (masculine) in Egypt. There may have been societies where social gender and physical sex were decoupled in this manner; however, social and physical gender are consistently equated in biblical Israel.

46. For an extensive review of the church fathers, from the early church to modern times, on sexual differentiation, see Christopher Chenault Roberts, *Creation and Covenant: The Significance of Sexual Difference in the Moral Theology of Marriage* (New York: T&T Clark, 2007).

47. Cf., Robert A. J. Gagnon, "Transsexuality and Ordination" (August, 2007; online at: www.robgagnon.net/articles/TranssexualityOrdination.pdf), 5–6.

48. Matthew Kuefler, *The Manly Eunuch: Masculinity, Gender Ambiguity, and Christian*

Ideology in Late Antiquity (The Chicago Series on Sexuality, History, and Society; Chicago: University of Chicago Press, 2001), 33.

49. Megan K. DeFranza, *Sex Difference in Christian Theology: Male, Female, and Intersex in the Image of God* (Grand Rapids: Eerdmans, 2015), 71.

50. For further discussion of the eunuch in Scripture and in church history, see DeFranza, *Sex Difference in Theology*, 68–106; Kuefler, *The Manly Eunuch*; Yarhouse, *Gender Dysphoria*, 32–5.

51. DeFranza, *Sex Difference in Theology*, 68.

52. Some societies artificially constructed a third gender category for the eunuch. For instance, "Byzantine society routinely gendered young eunuchs into patterns of behavior considered to be 'normal' for what it determined would be their gender category. … This resulted in the creation of a group of individuals that had all the attributes of a third gender." (Kathryn M. Ringrose, *The Perfect Servant: Eunuchs and the Social Construction of Gender in Byzantium* [Chicago: University of Chicago Press, 2013], 7.)

53. It has sometimes been held that Jesus called for literal castration of those wholly devoted to kingdom ministry, a view generally taken alongside literalistic readings of his instruction to cut of the offending hand or pluck out the offending eye (Matthew 5:29–30). These interpretations contradict the biblical importance of upholding bodily integrity (e.g., Deuteronomy 23:1). Jesus is upholding the eunuch's capacity for devotion to the household of Christ (cf., 1 Corinthians 7:6-8,28) as a model. In response to this error in certain quarters of the early church, the first canon of the Council of Nicea (A.D. 325) condemned self-castration.

54. Augustine, *The City of God against the Pagans* (trans. Eva Matthews Sanford and William McAllen Green; Loeb Classical Library, vol. 5; Cambridge: Harvard University Press, 1965), 16.8, 47.

55. Cf., LeFebvre, *Gospel and Sexual Orientation*, 38–40.

56. Roy E. Ciampa, cited by Megan K. DeFranza, *Sex Difference in Christian Theology: Male, Female, and Intersex in the Image of God* (Grand Rapids: Eerdmans, 2015), 177.

57. Raymond C. Ortlund, "Male-Female Equality and Male Headship: Genesis 1–3," in John Piper and Wayne Grudem, eds., *Recovering Biblical Manhood and Womanhood: A Response to Evangelical Feminism* (Wheaton, Ill.: Crossway, 1991), 95–112; Sam A. Andreades, *enGendered: God's Gift of Gender Difference in Relationship* (Wooster, Oh.: Weaver Book Company, 2015); Phyllis A. Bird, "'Male and Female He Created Them': Gen 1:27b in the Context of the Priestly Account of Creation," *Harvard Theological Review* 74.2 (1981), 129–59.

58. The language of dominion in this passage is not a license to abuse the world, any more than a king's dominion over his realm is justification for oppression.

59. What follows builds upon the discussion in LeFebvre, *Gospel and Sexual Orientation*, 23–8.

60. LeFebvre, *Gospel and Sexual Orientation*, 26.

61. See the discussion of Brain-Sex Theory in chapter I.

62. Peter A. Torjesen and Liv Sandnes, "Serum Testosterone in Women as Measured by an Automated Immunoassay and a RIA," *Clinical Chemistry* 50.3 (2004), 678.

63. "The Silicon Revolution," Europastar.com (2008), online at: www.europastar.com/ watch-knowledge/1003843153- the-silicon-revolution.html. Accessed Feb., 2017.

64. Christopher Exley, "Silicon in Life: A Bioinorganic Solution to Bioorganic Essentiality," *Journal of Inorganic Biochemistry* 69.3 (1998), 139–44.

65. Stanton L. Jones, "Is Sex or Gender a Choice?" in *The Holman Worldview Study Bible* (David S. Dockery and Jeremy Howard, eds.; Nashville: B&H Publishers, forthcoming).

66. "The sacred integrity of maleness or femaleness stamped on one's body." (Robert Gagnon, "Transsexuality and Ordination," www.robgagnon.net/articles/ TranssexualityOrdination.pdf.)

67. Peter A. Lee, et al, "Consensus Statement on Management of Intersex Disorders," *Pediatrics* 118.2 (2006), 1.

68. DeFranza, *Sex Difference in Theology*, 46.

69. Anne Fausto-Sterling, "The Five Sexes: Why Male and Female Are Not Enough," *The Sciences* (1993), 20–24; *Sexing the Body: Gender Politics and the Construction of Sexuality* (New York: Basic Books, 2000); DeFranza, *Sex Difference in Theology*, 44–6, 57–67.

70. Leonard Sax, "How Common is Intersex? A Response to Anne Fausto-Sterling," *The Journal of Sex Research* 39.3 (2002), 177.

71. Further discussion of known medical conditions leading to sexual ambiguity can be found in, Sax, "How Common is Intersex?," 175–7; DeFranza, *Sex Difference in Theology*, 25–44.

72. Of course, in biblical times it would not have been possible to examine internal organs. An individual born with AIS or CAH in ancient Israel could not consult the witness of internal anatomical features as we can, today, and may have continued for his or her entire life under a mistaken gender designation (although the development or lack of a particular physique might have prompted reflection). Nevertheless, we do not believe that biblical gender definitions require us to limit ourselves to biblical period technologies. The goal of following biblical guidance is not to make the same determination which an ancient Hebrew (with period technologies) would have made, but to make the right determination based on the divinely given doctrines of gender revealed through the ancient prophets. In those rare cases where anatomical ambiguity causes profound uncertainty, it is now possible to take into account many more facets of physical development than Bible-era families could have considered. Nevertheless, we are still upholding the same commitment to an *anatomically* based determination. We do not believe it is acceptable to regard neurological features (even when rooted in brain biology) as decisive in determining gender for the reasons discussed in connection with Brain-Sex Theory in chapter III.

73. Contra Augustine, *City of God*, 16.8, 47 (discussed in chapter III).

74. Even the medical establishment has begun to warn against the over-aggressive use of surgical procedures and the resulting physical and psychological impact. (E.g.,

Agius, "Intersex People: Issue Paper," 19–22.) The frequency with which irreversible "transition" is later regretted, and the rarity with which such "transition" brings real peace, has raised serious doubts about the whole prospect among some in the field, such as Paul R. McHugh, "Transgender Surgery Isn't the Solution: A Drastic Physical Change Doesn't Address Underlying Psycho-Social Troubles," *The Wall Street Journal*, June 12, 2014.

75. Capturing the spirit of the age, Oxford University Press recently published a series on *The Seven Deadly Sins*, re-assessing the status of each of these preeminent sins. In the volume in that series entitled *Lust*, Simon Blackburn argues that the time has come to rescue lust "from the denunciations of old men of the deserts, to deliver it from the pallid and envious confessor and the stocks and pillories of the Puritans, to drag it from the category of sin to that of virtue." (Simon Blackburn, *Lust: The Seven Deadly Sins* [New York: Oxford University Press, 2004], 3.)

76. Cf. Rosaria Champagne Butterfield, *Openness Unhindered: Further Thoughts of an Unlikely Convert on Sexual Identity and Union with Christ* (Pittsburgh, Pa.: Crown and Covenant, 2015), 52–8.

77. Paul's reference to praying "three times" may represent the idea of repeated prayer, rather than suggesting he only prayed about this matter on 3 occasions. (Calvin, *Calvin's Commentaries* [Grand Rapids: Baker, 2006], 20.2.376.)

78. Yarhouse, 148.

79. E.g., the first half of Recommendation #1, in, Agius, *Human Rights and Intersex*, 8.

80. Vaughan Roberts, *Transgender* (Purcellville, Va.: Good Book Company, 2016), 66. Emphasis original.

81. Mohler, *We Cannot Be Silent*, 82.

82. For the testimonies of those who regret having had sex-change procedures, see, www.sexchangeregret.com.

83. The so-called *Serenity Prayer* is relevant: "*God, grant me the serenity to accept the things I cannot change, Courage to change the things I can, And wisdom to know the difference.*" (P. R. McHugh, "Surgical Sex," *First Things* 147 [2004], 34.)

Other Titles from Crown & Covenant Publications

What Does the Bible Say about Homosexuality?

(3-panel brochure)

Secret Thoughts of an Unlikely Convert

Rosaria Butterfield

Openness Unhindered: Further Thoughts
of an Unlikely Convert on Sexual Identity
and Union with Christ

Rosaria Butterfield

The Book of Psalms for Worship

150 Questions about the Psalter

Bradley Johnston

Prayers of the Bible: 366 Devotionals to
Increase Your Prayer Life

Gordon J. Keddie

Crown & Covenant
PUBLICATIONS

The Gospel & Sexual Orientation

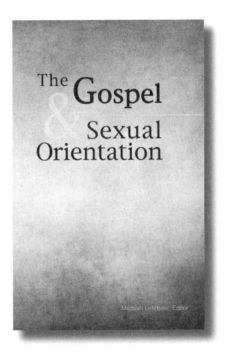

"Christians must avoid the stereotype of homosexuality as worse than all other sins and beyond the reach of God's grace."

Commissioned and later adopted by the Reformed Presbyterian Synod of 2011, this book provides guidance for congregations on the subject of homosexual orientation, not simply about the scriptural, scientific, and moral issues, but also for care and counsel to someone who believes their identity is homosexual. Interacting with contemporary scholarship and holding the Scriptures in high esteem, this work also presents a model of how to care for and walk alongside a person who is struggling with his or her sexual identity. Read this book and test it against what the Bible says. We hope it will encourage discussion in your local church as you share it with others.